Read-About® Holidays

Martin Luther King Jr. Day

By Trudi Strain Trueit

Reading Consultant
Cecilia Minden-Cupp, PhD
Former Director of the Language and Literacy Program
Harvard Graduate School of Education
Cambridge, Massachsetts

Children's Press®
A Division of Scholastic Inc.
New York Toronto London Auckland Sydney
Mexico City New Delhi Hong Kong
Danbury, Connecticut

Designer: Herman Adler
Photo Researcher: Caroline Anderson
The photo on the cover shows a child celebrating Martin Luther
King Jr. Day.

Library of Congress Cataloging-in-Publication Data

Library of Congress Cataloging-in-Publication Data
Trueit, Trudi Strain.
   Martin Luther King Jr. Day / By Trudi Strain Trueit.
      p. cm. — (Rookie read-about holidays)
   ISBN-10: 0-531-12459-2 (lib. bdg.)   0-531-11840-1 (pbk.)
   ISBN-13: 978-0-531-12459-8 (lib. bdg.)   978-0-531-11840-5 (pbk.)
   1. Martin Luther King Jr., Day—Juvenile literature. 2. King, Martin Luther,
Jr., 1929–1968—Juvenile literature. I. Title. II. Series.
   E185.97.K5T78 2006
   323.092—dc22   2006003959

CHILDREN'S PRESS, and ROOKIE READ-ABOUT®, and associated
logos are trademarks and/or registered trademarks of Scholastic Library
Publishing. SCHOLASTIC and associated logos are trademarks and/or
registered trademarks of Scholastic Inc.
1 2 3 4 5 6 7 8 9 10 R 16 15 14 13 12 11 10 09 08 07

Martin Luther King Jr. was a brave African American leader.

Martin hugs his wife, Coretta Scott King.

Martin Luther King Jr. was born on January 15th, 1929. His family nicknamed him M. L.

M. L. grew up in Atlanta, Georgia. M. L. had an older sister, Christine, and a younger brother, Alfred.

M. L. (front row right) with his parents, grandmother, brother, and sister

Coretta Scott King and the Kings' four children

King married Coretta
Scott in 1953. They had
four children.

After college, King
became a minister like
his father and grandfather
were. People called him
Reverend King or Dr. King.

African Americans did not have the same rights as white people in the 1950s. They could not go to the same schools as whites. They could not eat in the same restaurants. They could not even use the same drinking fountains.

A separate drinking fountain for African Americans in North Carolina during the 1950s

King giving a speech

King began to speak out against laws that treated people differently. He led peaceful marches. He gave powerful speeches.

King's most famous speech was called "I Have a Dream." He said he hoped that someday his children would live in a nation where the color of their skin would not matter.

King giving his most famous speech in Washington, D.C.

Lyndon Johnson

King's words helped change things. U.S. President Lyndon Johnson signed the Civil Rights Act in 1964. It gave all Americans equal rights. The Voting Rights Act of 1965 made sure that every adult American who wanted to vote could do so.

Many people agreed with King. Others were strongly against him. King was shot and killed on April 4, 1968.

King's funeral

January 2007

Sunday	Monday	Tuesday	Wednesday	Thursday	Friday	Saturday
	1	2	3	4	5	6
7	8	9	10	11	12	13
14	15	16	17	18	19	20
21	22	23	24	25	26	27
28	29	30	31			

A national holiday was created to honor King in 1983. It is the third Monday in January. Banks, schools, and post offices close on this day.

Ways to Celebrate

Many American schools hold special ceremonies the Friday before Martin Luther King Jr. Day. Students read essays about what civil rights mean to them. They talk about how to treat people of all races fairly.

Celebrating Martin Luther King Jr. Day in school

The "Let Freedom Ring" choir standing in front of
King's picture

Churches hold special services on Martin Luther King Jr. Day. People read out loud from King's speeches. Choirs and musical groups perform.

Some families visit museums on the holiday. They look at photos of King and the way life used to be before the Civil Rights Act. They may also watch videotape of King speaking.

Visitors to the National Civil Rights Museum in Memphis, Tennessee

Planting a peace garden in Florida

Martin Luther King Jr. Day is also a day to serve others. Many people pick up litter in their neighborhood. They plant trees in the park. They help feed and house the homeless.

Cities across America also hold parades and marches. People of all backgrounds walk together in memory of Martin Luther King Jr. and his dream.

Remembering Dr. King with a parade

Words You Know

choir

Coretta Scott King

marches

Martin Luther King Jr.   Lyndon Johnson

speeches

Index

About the Author

Trudi Strain Trueit is a former television news reporter and weather forecaster. She has written more than thirty fiction and nonfiction books for children. Ms. Trueit lives near Seattle, Washington, with her husband Bill.

Photo Credits